HOW TO MAKE A TON OF MONEY WITH AFFILIATE MARKETING

Become A Master At Affiliate Marketing

PATRICK KENNEDY

Contents

Introduction   v

Chapter 1   1
Chapter 2   4
Chapter 3   8
Chapter 4   13
Chapter 5   20
Chapter 6   23

Afterword   27

Introduction

This book will explain how to start affiliate marketing. If you continue to work at it, it is possible to make a 6-figure income.

I will show you explain what is affiliate marketing is and how you can effectively learn how to start your own business so that you will be earning passive income.

This is meant to be an easy step-by-step guide for affiliate marketing beginners with little to no experience online.

It's easy to read and understand without any of the technical verbiage so a beginner can get started with affiliate marketing easily.

Enjoy!

Chapter 1

What Is Affiliate Marketing?

ALTHOUGH MAKING money can be quite a challenge nowadays, this still does not change the fact that it is but essential especially given the current state of the economy. People have to work doubly hard in order to earn sufficient income to cover all their day to day expenses. And perhaps one of the consolations here is the fact that there are a couple of ways on how to generate income today, thanks to the Internet and information age.

The Internet has opened a lot of doors of money making opportunities to the public. And among the most popular of which today is affiliate marketing—which will be the center of discussion of this book.

To start off, what is affiliate marketing?

As Wikipedia put it, it is a marketing practice wherein a particular business or company rewards its affiliates for every visitor or customer that it is able to bring through marketing means.

So essentially, this means that if you work as an affiliate, your main goal will be to promote the products, services or brand of a certain business via the Internet. You will just to serve as the link or connection between the consumer and the seller. There is no need to create new products or service.

And if your marketing efforts are successful based on your ability to generate traffic to the website of your host company or business or a purchase, you will be given commission or pay according to the set terms.

Nonetheless, even though it sounds quite simple, it can still be quite tricky. Notice here that although this may be among the quickest and easiest ways, there is no mention of it being one of the easiest.

This is because affiliate marketing is a highly performance-driven type of marketing strategy. At the same time, the competition can be quite stiff especially given the intense competition among the businesses themselves, as well as the proliferation of other affiliate marketers who are contending for the same consumers.

There are also a couple of participants involved in the affiliate marketing process. To begin with, there is the merchant or company that hires the affiliate marketers in order to boost their sales and profits. Then there is you , the affiliate or publisher. You will be the one in charge of product, service or brand promotion. You will receive salary or commission depending on the results of your affiliate work.

In certain cases will be the network. It serves as the intermediate connection between the merchant and you, the affiliate. It processes the payments and provides various tools as well as offers.

Then last but certainly not least, there is the customer. He or she is your target market. Your ultimate goal is to make him or her buy the product of your host business after he or she has read the ad or review you have posted in your affiliate site.

THE BOTTOM LINE

Having said all that, the bottom line here is that affiliate marketing is all about product and brand promotion via the Internet. Ever since the latter has become an integral part of the lifestyle of the consumers in this generation, it has also become vital for the businesses to establish and maintain a strong presence in the World Wide Web. And one of the many ways to do this is through affiliate marketing.

As an affiliate marketer, your task will be to use your affiliate site to promote the products, services and brand of your host company. Although it may sound easy, it can be a bit tricky especially given the fact that there is a whole lot of other Internet marketers like you who are competing to get the attention of online shoppers.

Hence, you have to think about your own marketing tactic or strategy in order to stay ahead of the game. Since this is performance-based, the harder you work, the more money you will be able to earn.

Chapter 2

How Do I Get Started?

NOW THAT YOU have a general idea about what affiliate marketing is, the next step would be to know how it actually works. This will be the center of this chapter.

The first step to being an affiliate is choosing the affiliate program you want to be part of. In this area, there are lots to choose from especially since businesses are already appreciating the value of the internet in the success of their sales and profits. If you have a particular company in mind, just go straight to its site and see the requirements and processes for registration.

On the other hand, if you are still searching for possible choices, you can check out the Internet. Just use the search engines to look for affiliate programs and see the options in the search results page.

After you have chosen the business or company you prefer to work for, the next step would be to register your affiliate site or page. In some companies, this can be done for free, while others charge a certain fee.

Once your application has been approved, you can already pick out the products that you want to sell or market. Your host business will then provide you with an affiliate code that is unique for you. You will then use this to refer traffic to their website. This code will give them the signal that a particular customer made a purchase via your affiliate work. This will then be reflected in your performance and assessment for payment.

Ready-made promotional materials are also usually given by host companies. Most of the time, these are the same across all their affiliates to give a uniform look and branding. This way, they can instill brand recall among the consumers.

The promotional materials consist of text links, banners along with other types of creative copies. When you get them, all you have to do is copy the code and put it in your affiliate site. This is where traffic generation and referral will stem from.

So when your site visitors click on the links from your host site, they will be redirected to the latter. And when they make a purchase or subscription, the company will know that your affiliate site made the referral. Hence, you get commission.

As for performance monitoring of their affiliates, host businesses generate their own affiliate ID and affiliate software. An example of the latter will be the WP Affiliate Platform. At the same time, you will also be given a full and real time access to all the statistics related to sales and commission.

With all that, you already have everything that you need to do your affiliate work. Some companies can even provide custom-made creative materials for you. Just give them the specifics. This is usually done by those who wish to customize the promotional materials to fit the theme and elements of their affiliate site. This way, they can be more appealing and appropriate as well to the site's audience.

Once the creative materials have been provided for you, all that is left for you to do is plan an appropriate marketing strategy to reach your target market and persuade them to make a purchase, or just even show interest by clicking the link you have in your affiliate site.

Yes, there are times that you do not need to make a sale in order to get commission. Some host businesses provide different terms of payment. To give you an idea, here are some examples of affiliate payment terms:

PAY PER SALE. For one, there is the pay per sale option. Here, your merchant will pay you a certain percentage from the sale price once a client from your site completes a purchase. In this type, actual purchase from your referred client is necessary. Otherwise, you will have no commission.

PAY PER CLICK. For this particular type, no actual sale is necessary. You will get commission once a visitor from your site clicks one of the ads or links from your host company. So the more users clicking and being redirected to the site of your host company, the larger amount you will be paid.

PAY PER LEAD. Lastly, affiliates can also get payment once they are able to refer a visitor to the host site and get them to fill out a contact form. All you have to do is lead them to your host company's website and have them register and fill out a contact form. Once that process is completed, you will receive commission. Again, there is no need to make a sale.

Chapter 3

Why Become an Affiliate Marketer?

AFTER HAVING a short background on what affiliate marketing is and how it works, the next question to ask yourself now is why would you decide to become an affiliate marketer yourself? The fact is, there are a number of answers to that.

There are tons of benefits that you can derive from being involved in affiliate work as proven by the sheer number of people looking for affiliate marketing opportunities. You may have also read about the testimonials from other online entrepreneurs who made good money through becoming an affiliate marketer.

In this regard, you must know that this practice is already considered to be among the best fastest growing online income generating techniques in the world. That is why it is no surprise at all that a lot of both part timers and full timers are looking for work in this field.

Here are some of the reasons why you should also

consider a career as an affiliate marketer—whether on the side or as a full time job.

COST effective

To begin with, it is cost effective. You really do not have to spend a huge sum in order to be an affiliate marketer. There are even times that you do not have to spare a single dime at all such as in cases where registration is free.

Overall, Internet marketing is very much inexpensive. Take this for example. You do not have to worry over production cost because everything that you will need has already been developed by your host company. All the creatives, text links and other promotional materials will be supplied to you.

At the same time, everything is done via the Internet. Hence, you save quite a sum in terms of infrastructure and logistics. There is no need to pay for rent. Also, hiring employees and paying for their services is not necessary as well.

Global market

Since all transactions are done online, affiliate marketing gives you the chance to do business with people from all over the world. The Internet knows no physical boundaries. You can have clients from different countries all around the globe.

This means you can work as an affiliate in foreign companies. At the same time, you can cater to online consumers regardless of their geographic location. And with this extremely wide pool of clientele that you can tap into, there is a higher chance that you will get consumers to make a purchase or check out the products or services of your host company in order for you to get commission.

NO STORAGE and delivery

Another factor to love about affiliate marketing is that you do not need to fuss over details on storage, packing and shipping of products. All these will be taken care of by your host company or seller. This means less stress and hassle for you.

This is unlike the case when you are an online entrepreneur selling your own line of products or service. You have to worry about proper storage and packing of your products. You will also have to arrange shipping and other logistical support to have orders delivered to your client. In affiliate marketing, you do not have to worry about any of this. But just the same, you can still earn a huge sum of money.

NO NEED for customer support

In the same manner, affiliate marketers do not have to worry about customer support details. In fact, you do not even have to deal with consumer complaints at all since the seller or your host company is already the one in charge of that. You can continue with your work undisturbed.

So even if your referred clients encounter a problem or trouble with an item or service they availed of, you will have nothing to do with it. You do not have to provide assistance to them or any of that sort. The company will take care of that.

WORK FROM HOME

This is one of the perks of affiliate marketing that got a lot of hooked to it. In affiliate marketing, you can work in the comfort of your own home. There is no need to spend for gas, fare or food because you are already right in your abode where everything you need is available.

You do not have to fuss over getting stuck in traffic or rushing to go to work on your scheduled time in. Every transaction is done in the World Wide Web at the time that is most convenient for you. You are the master of your schedule so you can plan all your other activities accordingly.

PASSIVE INCOME

Last but certainly not least, this is another deal maker for a lot of people. By passive income, it means that even if you are not working, you still get to earn money because of the initial effort you have invested.

In regular jobs, you get a fixed salary as long as you are working within your shift or schedule. But in affiliate marketing, you can generate a steady flow of income even when you are far away from your computer and doing something else. It is all about your strategy and skill.

Once you have set up your marketing tactics, techniques and materials, you can already leave them and let them do their magic. All you have to do is monitor and check them out every once in a while. Know your progress. Then make an assessment. Of course, you should also upgrade your strategy on a regular basis so that it caters perfectly to the behavior and preferences of your target market.

Here are a few examples of websites that have made a good amount of their revenues with their affiliate marketing programs.

1. www.wanelo.com - which is now valued over $100 million(www.techcrunch.com)

2. www.geekalerts.com - uses mostly Clickbank and Amazon.com for affiliate marketing

3. www.thisiswhyimbroke.com - mostly uses the Amazon Affiliate marketing program

4. www.thewirecutter.com - recently valued at over $50 Million and still growing

---

Chapter 4

Seven Tips To Become An Effective Affiliate Marketer

UPON READING ALL the benefits that you can get from affiliate marketing, do not be too excited though. Yes, there are a lot to reap, but do not forget that you have to work for them. Do not ever entertain the misconception that you will be wealthy overnight from this racket.

Although this job can definitely be lucrative and also a great way make money via the Internet, it is also just as competitive. As mentioned earlier, there are a lot of other affiliate marketers out there who are competing for the exact same market that you are targeting.

Consistency is key to success with affiliate marketing.

You must be consistent when working affiliate marketing. If you are only going to put in 7 hours a week toward your affiliate marketing business, make it be 1 hour per

PATRICK KENNEDY

day, not 7 hours in one day because it comes through consistent application of marketing strategies. Set up a time each day to work on it and stick to your plan.

So for you to be a successful affiliate marketer, you have to understand a couple of things. This includes the needs of your target market, proper product promotion and other strategies that have been proven to work in the practice. To help you with that, here are some tricks that other successful affiliate marketers have applied and you might as well try for yourself, too.

CHOOSE ONLY a handful of good products

To begin with, you should be careful in your choice of products that you will promote or market. In this regard, one of the biggest mistakes commonly committed by new affiliate marketers—and even some of the old ones as well —is that they register with a whole lot of affiliate programs. Then they try to promote all the available products.

This is a big no-no. It will greatly affect your concentration, which in turn, will have an impact on your performance. It is like juggling a number of jobs. You cannot get a hold of them all. It will be too overwhelming. You will have your hands full and the chances are, you will not be able to promote even a single product properly.

While multitasking is possible, some people do not realize the dangers of overdoing it. Yes, you can register in more than one affiliate program and market a couple of items. But do not grab everything in sight.

You have to keep in mind that in order to be successful in this field, all you have to do is work with only a handful of good products—with emphasis on the good right there.

14

You will be amazed that even a little of these great products can already make you earn way more that what you can get if you promote a multitude of products.

This is because good products are not hard to sell. The consumers and shoppers themselves are the ones looking for ways to buy them. But of course, you still have to do your part and launch an equally good Internet marketing work. Keep in mind that there are a lot of other affiliate marketers competing for the same market.

So when you choose the products you will promote, the best practice is to know and understand the needs of your target market. At the same time, you should also search for goods that will perfectly align with the topic of your affiliate site.

This is a smart way of making money. You do not tire yourself too much, but still do the proper actions to get all the necessary work done and earn money.

USE a couple of traffic sources for product promotion

One of the common mistakes that some affiliate marketers commit is that they put advertisements and other promotional materials only in their sites. Although there is nothing wrong with this practice, you must also know that there are a lot of other sources that you can tap into in order to generate traffic and market products at the same time. It will be much better if you take a look at this for they will not only make your job easier, but also increase your chances of getting your clients to make a purchase. Keep in mind that the more traffic you generate to the host company's site and sales page, your chances of making a larger sum of money will also increase.

A good example that you can use is Google Adwords. Here, all you have to do is make an advertisement in your Adwords account. Afterwards, use the affiliate link provided to you and put it in the target page URL of the ad you made. Then you will have to measure the conversions continuously. It is important to see if the campaign you mounted costs less than the profit you are expecting to earn. If that is the case, then said campaign is definitely worth running.

TEST, measure and track your campaign

While using different strategies for product promotion is highly recommended, you must also not forget to monitor the progress of your project. This way, you will clearly see which techniques are giving you good results and which ones simply do not work. And with that, you can make an assessment to know what appropriate actions you should take.

In this regard, you can try split testing. This will help you adequately measure the performance of the campaigns you have mounted.

Once you get the results of the assessment, you can begin making some tweaks here and there. As studies and actual practice have shown, this can significantly increase your profits.

At the same time, it is also a good idea to put the banner advertisements in different areas in your site. Put them in various pages. And in each page, vary their locations as well. The underlying principle here is that some positions or areas will make the advertisements more conspicuous or noticeable than the others.

If your host company or affiliate program provides you basic statistics, make use of them. They will be helpful empirical data for your strategy planning. However, do not make the provided statistics serve as a limitation to you. Here are other conversions tracking software readily available for you. You can even make your own to track your affiliate campaign.

KEEP yourself and your campaigns updated

As mentioned earlier, the Internet has an ever-changing landscape. Hence, trends continuously change. With that, it is important that you as an affiliate marketer keep up with the latest techniques and strategies. Keep up with the times. Make sure that you know and understand the latest styles and tools in the marketing field. Otherwise, you will be left out while other affiliate marketers go on to progress.

So once you know the latest trends, plan your strategy around it. Observe and make an assessment. Keep in mind that you do not have to apply every new trend. Again, the ability to discern those that will work for you is important. Do not grab everything in sight.

Update your methods and techniques every now and then so that the consumers will not get bored. Keep in mind that they are constantly looking for something new. Hence, that is what you should give to them to catch their attention and investment.

WORK with the right merchant

Affiliate marketing has a lot to do with making the right choices. This is true not just in terms of products as discussed earlier, but also when it comes to merchants. Bear in mind that you will be marketing not just the products, but also the brand. Hence, you have to make it a point to pick a reputable company merchant. Again, smart choices.

You will also be putting your reputation on the line. When you put an ad in your affiliate site, it is already an outright personal recommendation to your visitors to patronize said brand or product. And of course, you do not want to disappoint your visitors by making them buy a particular product which made them unhappy eventually. With that, your credibility gets tarnished.

Every time this happens, less people will take your advice or recommendation. It lowers customer satisfaction. And that will hurt your reputation in the long run. If you plan to establish a career in affiliate marketing, that would signal your downfall.

So to avoid this, think wisely early on and work with credible companies and businesses. This way, you will be promoting good products that will be able to meet the demands of your clients. Hence, they will continue to patronize your site and this will be a good investment on your part.

PICK useful tools

Lastly, make things much easier for yourself by finding and using tools that will make your work more efficient. Remember, it is all about working smart. You do not have to tire yourself by working too hard if there are ways to achieve the same results with less work. One of which is through using Internet marketing tools. There are actually a lot of them out there.

Say for instance your affiliate site is powered by WordPress. You may as well consider getting a plug-in that is similar to the Affiliate Link Manager.

The bottom line here is that it will be much better for

you to devote your time searching for useful aids and tools then mastering them so you work more efficiently to achieve good results. This is the initial step. Then in the long run, you will see the benefits starting to manifest in terms of work convenience coupled with higher commission.

Chapter 5

Strategies To Generate Traffic

FOR THIS CHAPTER, you will be focused on generating traffic. Although this is the last, that does not mean that it is the least significant aspect of the job. Contrary to that, generating traffic is one of the first but most important steps in affiliate marketing.

But first, what does generating traffic mean? Essentially, it is about getting Internet users and consumers to visit the website or page of your host merchant. The traffic referred to here is the consumer traffic or the people visiting the website.

And in affiliate marketing, you should always take note of the fact that it is your job to get a whole lot of targeted traffic in order to be successful. At the same time, you should also keep in mind that not all the visitors of your affiliate site will click on the links and banner advertisements.

With that, it becomes much more important for you to

get more traffic by mixing and spicing up your marketing strategy. In this regard, you do not have to fret because there are actually a multitude of tactics that you can use. As a beginner, here are some that you can use.

SEARCH ENGINE OPTIMIZATION

Good rankings in search engine results pages lead to organic and highly targeted traffic that has higher chances of conversion. You could outsource SEO tasks, or do it yourself.

PAID advertising

For one, there is paid advertising. This strategy is deemed to be the most effective when the headline of your advertisement copy, graphics or message calling consumers to action just come together strongly in order to persuade consumers to click the links and make a purchase.

FREE ADVERTISING

Then there is free advertising. This is just like the first one, except that there are no fees. But of course, you cannot expect the same high quality and leeway. For this strategy, you can make use of sites like US Free Ads and Craigslist. These are two of the most famous sites that accept banner advertisements and links free of charge.

ARTICLE MARKETING

This is one of the most popular and widely used Internet marketing methods today. One reason for this is the fact that it offers quite a lot of benefits. For one, you will be building your reputation as a credible source in the niche you are working on. You will also gain a higher ranking in search engines as the number of links that lead to your site also increases. Given all that, more traffic will be generated to your affiliate site.

Chapter 6

Master Tools For Affiliate Marketing

NOW FOR THE FINAL CHAPTER, the tools for affiliate marketing. One thing you have to keep in mind about Internet marketing is that using specialized tools makes the job a whole lot easier and faster. With that, you become more efficient. More traffic is generated within a shorter period of time. That means your chances of reaching a quote or increasing your commission also rises.

But of course, you must also keep in mind that it is not just about using tools. You also have to pick the right tools for the job. To help you with that, here are some examples.

KEYWORD TOOLS

For one, there is the Google Keyword which was recently replaced with the Keyword Planner. This is among the most frequently used tools by affiliate marketers

—both newbies and veterans. Not only is it free, it is also very much effective. This Internet marketing tool provides valuable aid in the selection of keywords. This is very important in terms of Internet marketing.

Choosing and using the appropriate keywords is vital for Search Engine Optimization or SEO. This is one of the most important points budding affiliate marketers should know. Essentially, SEO is all about finding the right keywords and using them in the proper amounts in order to achieve higher ranking in search engines.

Now back to the Google Keyword / Keyword Planner. This tool helps you do research and analysis not just in terms of choosing appropriate keywords, but also when it comes to the proper manner in implementing them as well. As mentioned above, SEO does not stop with knowing the keywords, you must also use them carefully.

The Wordtracker is another free keyword tool that you can use. It works in pretty much the same way. But one difference is that you will have to give your contact details like name and email address in order to gain access to it.

On the other hand, if you are willing to shell out money, paid keyword tools will be a lot better. These are not as limited as their free counterparts. They also include more and better features.

For instance, they let their users dig deeper into their niche to come up with and compile a comprehensive collection of longtail keyword phrases. The latter will help you a lot in generating way more free traffic to your affiliate site.

The Wordtracker has a version for sale. You can also check out the Market Samurai, Wordstream, HitTail, Spyfu and the Keyword Spy. These are the more popular choices nowadays.

. . .

Plug-ins

Plug-ins are also extremely helpful. These are specially designed to automate particular tasks. That means, manual labor to be done by the affiliate marketer will be significantly lessened. Hence, you will be free to do other more important tasks. Here are some examples of the plug-ins that you can use.

For one, there is the Pretty Link Lite. As the name suggests, these make the dull affiliate links given to you "prettier" or more appealing. Hence, the links will better fit the overall look and theme of your site. Then they will become more persuasive to the site visitors.

You can also use the Duplicator. This lets you duplicate a blog of yours. That means when you need or want to come up with a new blog, you do not have to go through the same tedious process again. The plug-in will automatically duplicate every part of your blog.

Also a great plug-in is the Pinterest. This is among the most popular plug-ins today. Plus, it works very well for generating free traffic. But just the same, it is very easy to use. If someone "pins" an image that you own or which can be found in your site, the said image can easily become viral. That can eventually bring your affiliate page tons of visitors.

MARKET PROFILES

Last but certainly not least, there is the Market Profiles tool. This is among the most famous and in demand tools for affiliate marketing. It makes the process of targeting your market a whole lot easier.

All you have to do is put in specific information about the market that you want. Afterwards, the software will give you a score after analyzing through different indicators. The better the score you get, the nearer you are to succeeding within the specific niche being offered.

Afterword

I hope this book was able to help you to get a good idea about the basic concepts involved in affiliate marketing. The points stated and discussed in this book will be of great use to you as you start to venture in the promising field of affiliate marketing. Armed with the knowledge you got from this book, you will be able to do so much more to help you raise a great sum of money.

But of course, it does not end there. The next step is to apply the ideas that you have learned from the book. There is definitely no harm in trying. At the same time, you have to keep in mind that practice does make things perfect. You have to apply what you have learned in order to test if they will work for your case or not.

Nonetheless, you still have a free rein in coming up with your own strategy. You can tweak the ideas that you got from the book little by little until you find the perfect tactics that will work for you.

At the same time, you have to take note of the fact that this is a continuous learning process. Affiliate marketing is very dynamic especially given the ever-changing landscape of the World Wide Web today. Hence, you have to be highly flexible to accommodate changes and use them to your advantage.

www.ingramcontent.com/pod-product-compliance
Lightning Source LLC
Chambersburg PA
CBHW071532210326
41597CB00018B/2976